W9-BNS-418

FROM SEA to SHINING SEA

MAINE

CHRISTINE WEBSTER

Consultants

MELISSA N. MATUSEVICH, PH.D.
Curriculum and Instruction Specialist
Blacksburg, Virginia

MELISSA M. ORTH, M.L.A.
Young Adult Librarian
Curtis Memorial Library
Brunswick, Maine

CHARLENE SMITH WAGNER
Children's Librarian
Gardiner Public Library
Gardiner, Maine

CHILDREN'S PRESS®
A DIVISION OF SCHOLASTIC INC.

New York • Toronto • London • Auckland • Sydney • Mexico City
New Delhi • Hong Kong • Danbury, Connecticut

Maine is in the northeastern part of the United States. It is bordered by New Hampshire, Québec, New Brunswick, and the Atlantic Ocean.

The photograph on the front cover shows lobster and crab traps on the pier at Beals Island Harbor.

Project Editor: Meredith DeSousa
Art Director: Marie O'Neill
Photo Researcher: Marybeth Kavanagh
Design: Robin West, Ox and Company, Inc.
Page 6 map and recipe art: Susan Hunt Yule
All other maps: XNR Productions, Inc.

Library of Congress Cataloging-in-Publication Data

Webster, Christine.
    Maine / Christine Webster.
      v. cm. — (From sea to shining sea)
Includes bibliographical references and index.
Contents: Introducing the Pine Tree State—The land of Maine—Maine through history—
Governing Maine—The people and places of Maine—Maine Almanac—Timeline—Gallery
of famous people.
    ISBN 0-516-22323-2
    1. Maine—Juvenile literature. [1. Maine.] I. Title. II. Series.
    F19.3 .W43 2003
    974.1—dc21   2002001491

TABLE of CONTENTS

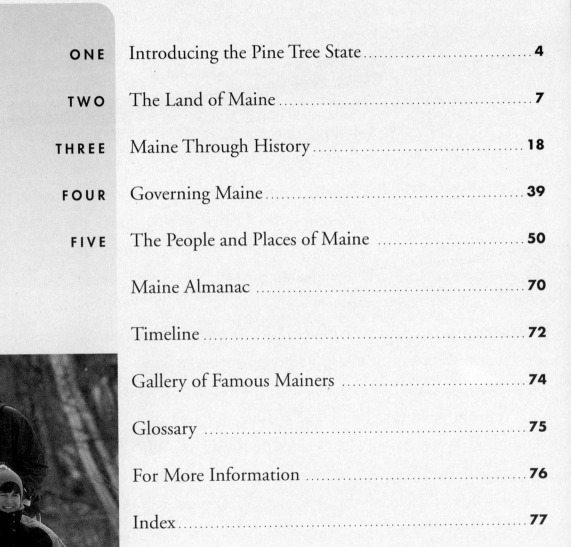

CHAPTER ONE

INTRODUCING THE PINE TREE STATE

Colorful lobster boats
brighten Bass Harbor
on Mount Desert Island.

Imagine being the first in the country to see the sun rise each morning. Residents of Maine enjoy this luxury. Maine greets the dawn before any other state because it forms the northeastern tip of the United States. Because the sun rises in the east, the state of Maine enjoys it first.

Maine is located in part of the United States known as New England. It ranks thirty-ninth in size among other states and is the largest of the six New England states. In fact, you could almost squeeze the rest of New England—Connecticut, Massachusetts, New Hampshire, Rhode Island, and Vermont—inside Maine. It is 322 miles (518 kilometers) long and 207 miles (333 km) wide.

Early settlers relied on the abundance of natural resources in Maine. In early days, Native Americans and colonists used the fine fishing grounds to survive. Later, settlers turned to Maine's dense forests.

Almost all of Maine is covered with forests, so it's no wonder the state's nickname is the Pine Tree State. Thanks to these resources, Maine grew to become an important shipbuilding center where sleek wooden sailing ships were made.

Today, Mainers still value these natural resources. Considered one of the most healthful states to live in, Maine offers easy access to fresh ocean air, forested mountains, and miles of uninterrupted wilderness. Maine still relies on wood for its economy. It is also the nation's top producer of blueberries, ranks sixth in the production of potatoes, and harvests more than 57 million pounds of lobster each year!

What comes to mind when you think of Maine?

❖ Enormous wooden ships sailing in and out of seaports

❖ Henry Wadsworth Longfellow penning poetry

❖ Tiny boats unloading huge traps filled with their daily catch of lobsters

❖ Large moose roaming the land

❖ Billions of manufactured toothpicks and other wood products

❖ Seventy-two lighthouses to guide ships

❖ Hot air balloons over Lewiston and Auburn during the Great Falls Balloon Festival

❖ Hikers enjoying the view from Mt. Katahdin

Maine has a rich history and promises a bright future. Discover the culture, history, and beauty of the Pine Tree State. Turn the page to discover Maine!

Presque Isle

Bangor

Augusta

Bar Harbor

Portland

ATLANTIC OCEAN

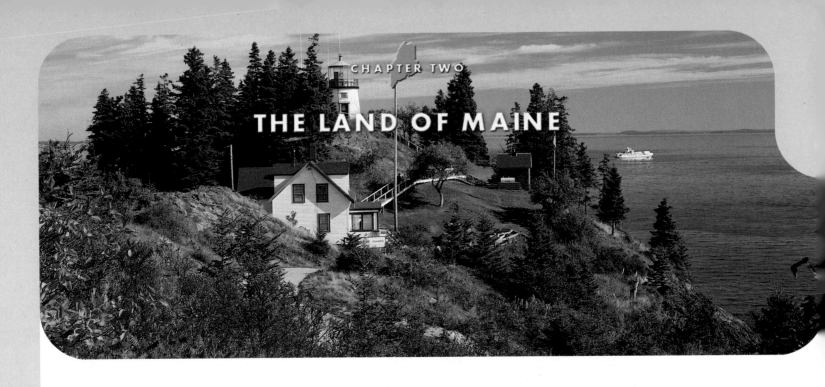

CHAPTER TWO

THE LAND OF MAINE

Maine forms the northeastern tip of the United States. On a map, Maine looks like a wedge between two Canadian provinces: New Brunswick and Québec. New Brunswick is to the northeast, and Québec is to the northwest. Maine is the only state bordered by just one American state; New Hampshire is southwest of Maine. The Atlantic Ocean forms the southeast border.

As the largest of the six New England states, Maine covers 35,387 square miles (91,652 square kilometers). The coastline stretches more than 228 miles (367 km). If you include deep harbors, coves, and bays, it reaches a length of 3,478 miles (5,597 km).

Maine is famous for having a beautiful coastline dotted with lighthouses. Owl's Head Lighthouse, above, is in Owl's Head, Maine.

GEOGRAPHIC REGIONS

Millions of years ago, during what is known as the Ice Age, Maine was covered with thick glaciers, or sheets of ice. The glaciers

7

The rocky shoreline of Casco Bay provides nesting areas for waterbirds and a unique habitat for many other animals.

smoothed and rounded the hills and mountains, filled the lakes and rivers, and pushed around rocks and boulders. As a result of the glaciers' movement, there are three distinct natural regions in Maine today: the Coastal Lowlands, the Eastern New England Upland, and the White Mountains Region.

Coastal Lowlands

The Coastal Lowlands form a strip along the Atlantic Ocean shoreline, extending 10 to 40 miles (16 to 64 km) inland. These lowlands consist of gently rolling terrain, but in some areas there are rugged mountains and steep hills. The coast of Maine is mostly rocky, but there are sandy beaches along the southern coastline. Many bays, inlets, and coves indent the northern coast, while rocky cliffs jut into the ocean.

More than 2,000 islands speckle the Atlantic Ocean off the coast of Maine. Mount Desert is the largest, at 110 square miles (285 sq km). Much of this island makes up part of Acadia National Park, a popular tourist area. Many of Maine's islands are charming to visit and are popular tourist areas in summer. One such island includes the 700-acre (283-hectare) Monhegan Island. Regular ferries can travel to this modern fishing village in about an hour. Lying off the coast of Portland in Casco Bay is Long Island. This small island—only 2.75 miles (4.4 km) long and .75 miles (1.2 km) wide—has 202 residents and many visitors, all of whom can enjoy bicycling, rock climbing, and spectacular sunsets on the island.

Most mines are on the coast. Granite, limestone, and sand are important mineral resources found there. Granite is a hard rock that is used to make buildings. Limestone is used to make cement.

Fishermen sail from many ports along the coast. Lobster, tuna, cod, flounder, and shellfish swim off the coastal waters. Small farms in the area raise beef and poultry, and grow blueberries.

EXTRA! EXTRA!

The largest tidal whirlpool in the Western Hemisphere is Old Sow, between Deer Island, New Brunswick, and Moose Island in Maine. A tidal whirlpool is a body of water that spins in a circular motion. The motion may be caused by the meeting of two countercurrents (two currents flowing in the opposite direction), the wind, or irregularities at the bottom of the water. At Old Sow, the water flows in and out so often (every six hours) that the area comes alive with boils, ripples, and whirlpools. Water sometimes sprays 12 to 20 feet (3.6 to 6 meters) in the air!

Monhegan Island is small enough that there are no cars or paved roads on the island.

9

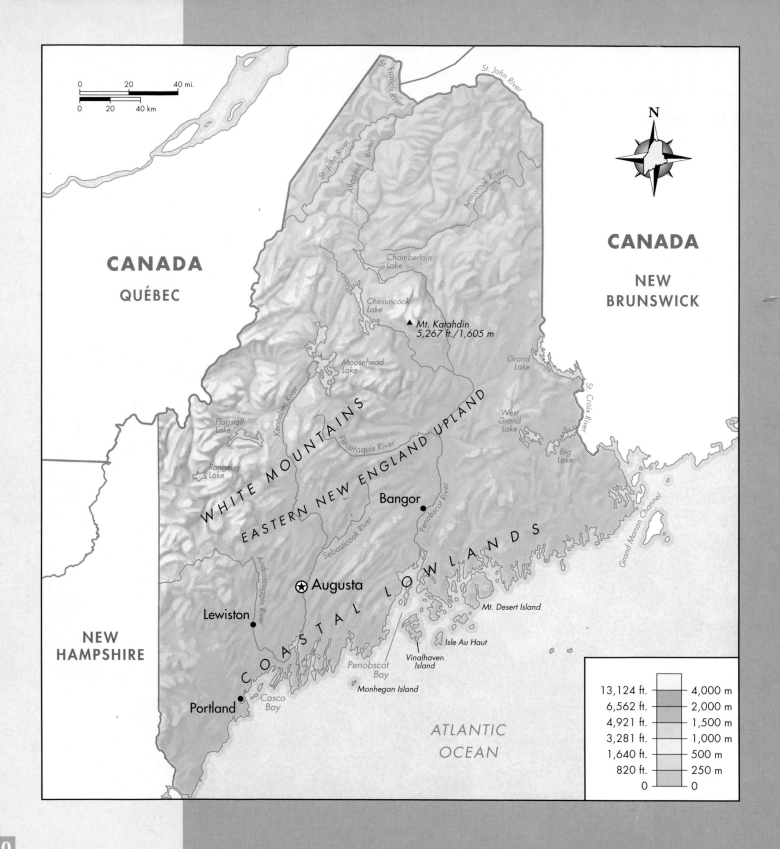

0 20 40 mi.
0 20 40 km

N

CANADA
QUÉBEC

St. Francis River

St. John River

CANADA

NEW
BRUNSWICK

St. John River

Allagash River

Aroostook River

Chamberlain
Lake

Chesuncook
Lake

▲ Mt. Katahdin
5,267 ft./1,605 m

Grand
Lake

Moosehead
Lake

St. Croix River

Kennebec River

WHITE MOUNTAINS

EASTERN NEW ENGLAND UPLAND

West
Grand
Lake

Flagstaff
Lake

Piscataquis River

Big
Lake

Rangeley
Lake

Bangor

Penobscot River

Sebasticook River

COASTAL LOWLANDS

Grand Manan Channel

Androscoggin River

⊛ Augusta

Lewiston

Mt. Desert Island

Isle Au Haut

NEW
HAMPSHIRE

Vinalhaven
Island

Penobscot
Bay

Portland

Casco
Bay

Monhegan Island

ATLANTIC
OCEAN

13,124 ft.	4,000 m
6,562 ft.	2,000 m
4,921 ft.	1,500 m
3,281 ft.	1,000 m
1,640 ft.	500 m
820 ft.	250 m
0	0

Eastern New England Upland

The Eastern New England Upland is located northwest of the Coastal Lowlands. It forms a strip through the middle of Maine. The Eastern New England Upland rises from sea level in the east to nearly 2,000 feet (610 m) in the southwest. It is the largest natural region in the state.

The Eastern New England Upland consists of rolling hills and dense forests. Mountains cut through the center of this region, averaging 1,100 to 1,250 feet (340 to 380 m) in elevation. Many lakes and rivers are found in this area, including Moosehead Lake, Maine's largest lake. This irregular-shaped lake is 35 miles (56 km) long and up to 10 miles (16.1 km) wide. Mount Kineo stands 1,789 feet (545 m) high on a peninsula that extends into the lake.

The Aroostook Plateau is found in the northeastern part of this region. This plateau of high, level, flat land contains rich and fertile soil that is suitable for farming. Potato, dairy, and beef farms dot the Aroostook Plateau. Maine's famous potatoes are grown there.

Mount Kineo and Moosehead Lake are popular recreation areas for Mainers.

White Mountains Region

The White Mountains region covers the north and northwestern parts of Maine. The White Mountains are part of a large chain called the Appalachian Mountains, which stretches from southeastern Canada to central Alabama. The range called the White Mountains reaches across northwestern Maine and into New Hampshire and Vermont.

The White Mountains region is the most rugged and thickly forested area of Maine. It includes hundreds of lakes and most of Maine's highest mountains, including the state's highest peak, Mount Katahdin (5,267 feet/1,605 m). Mt. Katahdin is also the final stop on the 2,160-mile (3,476-km) Appalachian Trail, a footpath that runs from Georgia to Maine. In summer, visitors to the Mt. Katahdin area

Mount Katahdin is located within Baxter State Park.

can go kayaking, whitewater rafting, or canoeing. Winter activities include snow-mobiling, snowshoeing, cross-country skiing, and ice fishing.

Other mountains in this area reach elevations of 4,000 feet (1,219 m). Most of Maine's mountains look green all year because they are covered by fir trees. All of these trees provide raw material for Maine's largest manufacturing industry—paper and wood products.

EXTRA! EXTRA!

In 1846, famous American writer and naturalist Henry David Thoreau climbed Mount Katahdin. After exploring the backwoods of Maine, Thoreau was so inspired that he wrote three essays about his adventures. They were later published as a book titled *The Maine Woods*.

PLANTS AND ANIMALS

Much of Maine, particularly the northern half, is covered by forests. Valuable trees include the white pine, balsam fir, basswood, maple, oak, and spruce. Most of the commercial forests (forests whose trees are harvested and sold) are privately owned by companies for making lumber or paper. Maine trees also provide a healthy portion of the nation's maple syrup.

The tree-covered hillsides in Baxter State Park turn beautiful colors in autumn.

Moose are plentiful in Maine.

Witch hazel blankets the forests and box alder flourishes among Maine's thick swamps. Flowers include lupine, black-eyed Susans, meadow lilies, and anemones. All are common in Maine and other northeastern states.

Maine has a diverse wildlife population compared to other New England states. Many kinds of birds, such as eagles, sparrows, owls, seagulls, and chickadees, fly through Maine's skies. The chickadee is Maine's state bird. Although many of these birds are found throughout the northeast, they occupy Maine's skies daily.

The Pine Tree State has more moose than any other state besides Alaska. About 25,000 moose live in the Maine woods. These animals can weigh up to 1,800 pounds (816 kilograms)—about the weight of eight men put together! Among the larger animals found in Maine's thick forests are black bears, lynxes, bobcats, and white-tailed deer. Small animals such as beavers, foxes, mice, chipmunks, voles, rabbits, and minks also live in Maine.

Maine has more than 5,000 rivers and streams. Most of the rivers in Maine run from north to south. The St. John is the most important river in northern Maine. Major hydroelectric power plants (places in which flowing water is used to create electricity) are found along its shores. It flows northeast along Maine's northern border with New Brunswick before entering Canada. The St. John and St. Croix rivers form part of the international boundary with Canada.

Three of Maine's major rivers include the Androscoggin, the Kennebec, and the Penobscot. The Androscoggin River rises at the border of New Hampshire, and flows southward until it joins the Kennebec. The Kennebec River begins in central Maine as an outlet of Moosehead Lake, and flows south into the Atlantic Ocean, near Bath. The Penobscot River flows east and south from the lakes of north central Maine and empties into Penobscot Bay, south of Bangor.

Maine has 2,500 lakes and ponds. These include the Chesun-

The Penobscot River is a popular place for white-water rafting.

cook, the Chamberlain, Grand, and Spednic lakes. The Rangeley Lakes in southwestern Maine are a popular vacation area.

Maine's rivers, lakes, and streams provide homes for smallmouth bass, landlocked salmon, and brook trout. Lobsters, clams, and shrimp swim off the coastal waters, along with cod and flounder.

CLIMATE

Maine enjoys four distinct seasons with comfortable summers and long winters. July temperatures average 70° Fahrenheit (21° Celsius). Summers are short; the leaves on trees start to change color as early as August. The hottest day ever recorded in Maine was on July 10, 1911, at North Bridgton, when temperatures soared to 105° F (41° C).

Winters in Maine are cold, and temperatures can dip as low as –20° F (–29° C). In northern Maine, residents may get up to 100 inches (254 centimeters) of snow in one season! The climate is generally milder along the coast, especially in winter. The coldest day ever recorded in Maine was on January 19, 1925, at Van Buren, when temperatures dipped to a chilly –48° F (–44° C).

Maine's shores are usually cool because of the Arctic air and coastal winds from the Labrador Current. The Labrador Current is a cold ocean current that rises from the Arctic Ocean off the shores of Labrador, Canada. When it meets with warm air

EXTRA! EXTRA!

While the four seasons—spring, summer, fall, and winter—are common in the Northeast, Mainers sometimes count a fifth season: mud season. Mud season starts in April, after winter weather ends and before spring weather starts. The snow melts and the spring rain falls, leaving the earth damp, messy, and full of—mud!

above the Gulf Stream, heavy fog occurs off the coast of Maine. Maine's many lighthouses help water vessels to see through the heavy fog.

Fog is frequent and heaviest along the coast, when cold air from the ocean meets warm air on land. The Pine Tree State gets 40 to 46 inches (101 to 116 cm) of rain per year. The coastal areas are somewhat wetter than other areas.

Strong storms sometimes blow in from the northeast and create enormous waves. The storms, called northeasters (or nor'easters), bring snow, rain, and gusty winds. These storms are usually created during the late fall, winter, and early spring. Besides the messy weather, severe flooding often occurs along the coast.

EXTRA! EXTRA!

In January 1998, an ice storm paralyzed Maine. The storm knocked down trees and power lines and covered some areas with three inches (7.6 cm) of ice. Some places had no power for two weeks, leaving residents shivering in the freezing temperatures. As a result, former President Clinton declared Maine a federal disaster area.

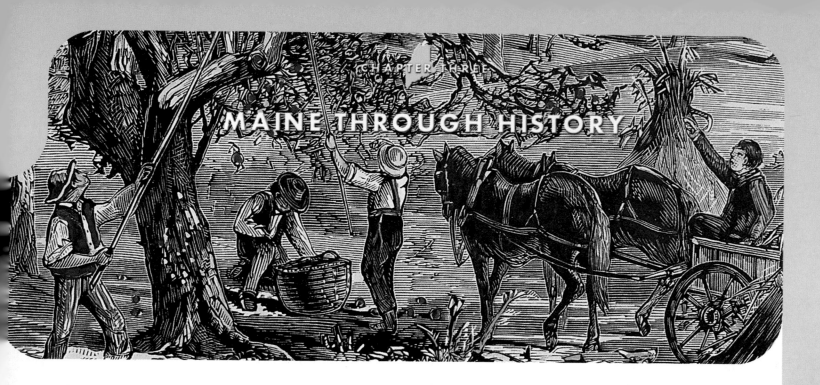

CHAPTER THREE

MAINE THROUGH HISTORY

Many of Maine's early settlers grew apples for their own use or for sale in local markets.

About **12,000 years ago, Paleo-Indians** were the first humans in Maine. It is believed they arrived in Maine from Asia, by traveling over the Bering Land Bridge into Alaska, through Canada and into what is now the United States. They used hand-crafted spears to hunt large animals such as caribou, wooly mammoths, giant bisons, and musk ox. Over time, the Paleo-Indians disappeared, possibly due to a change in Maine's climate.

After the Paleo-Indians disappeared, about 4000 to 1000 B.C., the Red Paint People arrived. Archaeologists gave them this name because red *ocher* was found inside their underground graves. Ocher is a reddish-brown clay that was smeared on people's bodies, huts, and possessions. The Red Paint People sharpened stones to make arrowheads and spears for hunting deer and fish. Their remains suggest that they settled throughout Maine. They disappeared for unknown reasons.

About 1500 B.C., the Susquehanna tradition developed in the Maine area. This new culture migrated farther from the coast, to the interior. As a result, they depended more on the land than on water to find food. Their population also declined for no known reason.

Several centuries later, around 500 B.C., there were two groups of Native Americans living in Maine: the Micmac and the Abenaki. Both tribes were once part of a larger group called the Wabanaki. At one time there were almost twenty tribes within the Wabanaki group, including today's Passamaquoddy, Penobscot, Micmac, and Maliseet tribes. The Micmac, who lived in eastern Maine, were enemies of the Abenaki. However, the Abenaki outnumbered the Micmac, so the Micmac stayed around eastern Maine to avoid conflict.

The Abenaki occupied most of the state. They were a large group whose name means "people of the dawn." The Abenaki respected the land and animals. They farmed and fished to survive, and moved often to find the best sources for food. The Abenaki grew fields of corn and beans, and gathered edible plant roots. In spring they collected sap from maple trees to be made into maple syrup. They even had pet dogs for watching and protecting their homes. The Abenaki lived in cone-shaped wigwams built with birch bark frames and covered with animal skins.

At one time, the Abenaki population was believed to reach 20,000, but many died from disease or war after the Europeans arrived. Of the

Early Native Americans made their homes from bent saplings covered with animal skins.

dozens of tribes that once lived in Maine, only four remain today: the Passamaquoddy, Penobscot, Micmac, and Maliseet. The Penobscot and Passamaquoddy nations have nonvoting representatives within the state government. (A nonvoting representative belongs to the state house of representatives, but cannot vote.) As they were once the first people on Maine's land, they are still active residents in the Pine Tree State.

EUROPEAN EXPLORERS ARRIVE

The first known European explorer in Maine was Giovanni da Verrazano, an Italian explorer sailing under the French flag in 1524. Verrazano traveled along Maine's coast, writing reports on the land and people for the king of France. Although he made no attempt to establish a colony, he claimed the region for France.

England also sent several explorers to Maine. Each explorer provided information to England about Maine's land, waters, and people. It wasn't long before European fishing vessels began arriving to take advantage of the rich fishing grounds off the coast of Maine. Fishermen salted or sun-dried their catches before taking them back to Europe.

France's first colony in Maine was founded by Pierre du Guast and Samuel de Champlain in 1604. A group of about seventy people settled on an island at the mouth of the St. Croix River, which now forms part of the border between Maine and Canada. The winter was not kind to this colony. Nearly all the settlers froze to death and their supplies almost ran out. The colony lasted less than one year, and the survivors moved to Nova Scotia (Canada) or returned to France.

Giovanni da Verrazano was the earliest known European explorer to visit Maine.

EXTRA! EXTRA!

Some scientists think that Leif Ericson, a Norse explorer, arrived in Maine before Giovanni da Verrazano. They believe Ericson led a crew of Vikings to the area around A.D. 1100. However, there is little proof that the Vikings ever reached Maine or even North America. The only evidence is a single Norse coin found in Maine in 1961. The coin may have come from trading among the natives.

Samuel de Champlain explored parts of the northeastern coast, including New York and Massachusetts.

The most notorious exploration was by George Waymouth in 1605. Two wealthy Englishmen, Sir Ferdinando Gorges and Sir John Popham, sent Waymouth to explore Maine for the possibility of settlement. He scoured the coast and, just as he was about to sail back to England, he kidnapped five Native Americans. He forced them to travel back to England in hopes that they could describe the rich land of Maine. Gorges and Popham questioned the Native Americans, who used gestures to describe their beautiful lands. The Native Americans convinced the English that this faraway land could be valuable. As a result, many English headed to Maine in search of wealth.

In 1607 Popham's nephew, George Popham, brought a group of colonists to Maine. They set up a colony, named the Popham Plantation, at the mouth of the Kennebec River. There the colonists built a ship called the *Virginia*. The ship was 50 feet (15 m) long. It was the first ship built by the English in the New World that would sail to Europe. The Popham Plantation lasted only one year. Cold winter weather, deaths of the colony's leaders, and Native American attacks forced the settlers to return to England in the spring of 1608.

Native Americans felt threatened by the Europeans. Many were dying from diseases such as smallpox and tuberculosis that had been brought by European settlers. Native Americans also felt that the new colonists were trying to take their land.

In 1613 the French returned. Four Jesuit priests established a mission on Mount Desert Island in order to teach the Christian religion to

French missionaries arrived on Mount Desert Island in 1613.

Native Americans. The missionaries also planned to fish for cod, which was plentiful in Maine's waters, and trap foxes, minks, and beavers, whose valuable furs could be taken back to Europe to be made into capes and hats. However, the commander of an English fishing group, Sir Samuel Argall, ordered the French to leave. The Englishmen declared that the island belonged to England and they destroyed the French settlement. This conflict, and others like it, set the stage for eventual war between the French and the English.

More settlements were established along the Maine coast, but few could survive the cold winters and Native American attacks. Many battles were fought in Maine in its early days. Native Americans fought the

Trading was common between Native Americans and Europeans. Animal skins were offered in exchange for European goods, such as muskets and iron kettles.

British (English), and the French and British fought over land rights. Although Native Americans traded with both the French and British, they often sided with the French because they were more accepting of their way of life.

The first permanent English settlements were established at Monhegan in 1622, Saco in 1623, and Agamenticus (present-day York) in 1624. In 1622, King James I of England gave land in North America to Sir Ferdinando Gorges and his partner, John Mason. This large tract of land included today's Maine and part of New Hampshire. Seven years later, in 1629, Gorges and Mason divided their land. Gorges took the eastern part and called it Maine, after a province in France. (The name may have also been chosen to distinguish the mainland from the offshore islands.) Mason took the western part and named it New Hampshire.

Although Sir Ferdinando Gorges never came to Maine, he set up the area's first government in 1636 and appointed officials to govern. Five years later, he changed the name of Agamenticus to Georgeana. It became the first chartered English city in the United States.

After Sir Ferdinando Gorges died in 1647, the towns of Kittery, Wells, and York united under a new government. Ownership disputes developed over Maine, and between 1652 and 1658 the Massachusetts Bay Colony claimed parts of the territory, including Kittery, Wells, and York. Then, the family of the late Sir Ferdinando Gorges decided to sell its land in Maine to Massachusetts. From 1677 to 1820, Maine was considered part of Massachusetts.

THE FRENCH AND INDIAN WAR

Land disputes occurred in other areas, as well. Both the English and the French wanted to claim ownership of the New World territories. Maine was attractive because of its fur trade and rich fishing areas. From 1754 to 1763, the French and Indian War raged in North America. Many battles between the English and French were fought throughout the New England area and Canada. The battles destroyed several of Maine's towns, and many people died as a result.

The war ended with the signing of the Treaty of Paris in 1763, which gave England control of most of North America. Many Abenaki fled to Canada. Only a small

The French and the British fought for control of North American territory during the French and Indian War.

25

number stayed in Maine. Eventually, the remaining Penobscot, Passamaquoddy, Micmac, and Maliseet were forced to move to land that was reserved, or set aside for them, called a reservation. Today, about 1,500 Passamaquoddy live on two reservations. The largest, located near Eastport, is called the Pleasant Point Indian Reservation. The other is located just above Princeton and is called Indian Township Reservation. There are about 1,200 Penobscot living on Indian Island, 482 Micmac in Aroostook County, and 554 Maliseet near Houlton.

After the war, settlers returned once again to rebuild forts. From 1765 to 1775, the population of Maine increased from 23,000 to 47,000. Like the Native Americans before them, these new settlers used the natural resources of Maine. The dense forests provided wood for timber and shipbuilding, while the waters provided an abundance of fish for food. As more settlers arrived, farming gained importance. Cows were raised for milk and butter, and corn was an important crop for many years.

THE AMERICAN REVOLUTION

Although the war was over, Great Britain was still paying for it. In order to raise money, Great Britain raised taxes (extra charges) on paper products in the colonies during the 1760s. They also added taxes on products such as tea and stamps. As part of Massachusetts, Maine was one of the thirteen English colonies and was subject to the taxes.

The taxes angered people throughout the colonies. They felt they were being unfairly taxed, because the colonies were not represented in the English government. People could be heard shouting, "No taxation without representation!" Taxation was only one problem, however. Many colonists also felt that British rule was repressive and strict. As time went by, a growing number of colonists, called patriots, wanted complete freedom from British rule.

Falmouth suffered a brutal attack before the onset of the American Revolution.

Hundreds of Mainers joined Massachusetts patriots to protest the taxes. They ran tax collectors out of town and boycotted British goods, refusing to buy, sell, or barter them. In October 1774, a group of angry patriots in Maine burned the supply of British tea stored at York. To punish the people for opposing the king's rules, the British navy burned Falmouth (now Portland) the following year. British ships also blocked trade in Maine, which meant that goods could not come or go from Maine. This caused a shortage of food and other necessities.

On June 12, 1775, colonists captured a British warship called the *Margaretta* in Maine's Machias Bay. This attack is considered the first naval battle of the American Revolution (also called the Revolutionary

War, 1775–1783). After the captain of the *Margaretta* was injured, the British surrendered the ship.

One of the most disastrous naval battles of the war also occurred in Maine. During the Penobscot Expedition in 1779, the British took over the town of Castine on the Penobscot River. Although the town's residents did not protest the presence of British soldiers, Massachusetts sent ships to reclaim Castine. When the British learned that Americans were on their way, they sent more ships, easily defeating American forces. Some sailors ran into the forests, while others burned their own ships rather than allow the British to take them. The coast of Maine remained under British control until the American Revolution ended in 1783. As a result of the war, the thirteen colonies won independence from Great Britain and formed their own government as the United States.

INDUSTRIAL DEVELOPMENT

After the war, Maine prospered thanks to its thick white pine forests. A huge logging industry developed, and the logs were used to make ships' masts. In turn, the logging industry fueled the shipbuilding industry. Some of the finest ships in the world were built in Maine. The ships also helped to develop Maine's fishing industry. The waters off the coast of Maine teemed with cod, halibut, and lobster. Cod had been important to Maine's economy since colonial days, and it was Maine's primary export until the nineteenth century.

Maine was famous for making sleek wooden sailing vessels.

Farming continued to grow and by 1820, potatoes had replaced corn as the number one crop. Potatoes grew well in the valleys of Aroostook, Kennebec, and Penobscot. However, Mainers continued to rely on lumber—the state's largest industry—to earn a living.

In 1836, Maine's first railroad was completed. It was used to carry lumber to Bangor and Old Town. Some lumber was used to build ships, and some was sold to other states. Lumberjacks lived in the forests and cut down large logs. In winter, they hauled the logs by sled and piled them next to the Kennebec and Penobscot rivers. In spring, when the ice broke up, lumberjacks put the logs in the water to let river currents carry them to sawmills downstream.

Paper mills opened in towns such as Westbrook and Yarmouth. Many of these mills used hydroelectric power, in which the force of water is used to create electricity to run machines. Hydroelectric plants

This drawing shows a sawmill on the Penobscot River in the 1850s. Sometimes the river was so crowded with logs that people could walk across them from one shore to the other.

were built on the Androscoggin, Kennebec, Penobscot, and Saco rivers. Water-powered factories sprang up beside the sawmills along Maine's rivers.

Cotton and woolen textiles emerged in the 1840s as an important industry in Maine. Fibers separated from the seeds of cotton or sheep's wool were processed in mills (factories) to make cloth. Many French-Canadians were lured by the opportunity to work in these mills and migrated to Maine. The production of textiles, paper, and leather products all became major sources of employment.

STATEHOOD

Meanwhile, in part because Massachusetts had been unable to protect Maine against British raids during the American Revolution, Mainers pushed for separation from Massachusetts. They wanted to form a state of their own. On March 15, 1820, Maine became the twenty-third state. Portland was its first capital and William King, a prominent merchant and shipbuilder, became governor. There were 300,000 people living in Maine at this time. The new state had 236 towns and 9 counties. In 1832, the capital moved to Augusta because of its central location.

Maine was admitted to the Union as part of the Missouri Compromise. The Missouri Compromise was an agreement created by Congress to keep the number of slave states equal to that of free states (states without slaves). Maine entered the Union as a free state so that Missouri could enter as a slave state.

Slavery began in the colonies in the 1600s, when Europeans kidnapped Africans from their home country and sold them to American colonists. In the colonies, slaves were forced to perform hard labor, usually on farms. Eventually, slavery developed into a profitable business, as slaves were bought and sold among landowners. Slaves were often treated cruelly and they had no rights as individuals. They were mainly used in the southern colonies, where they worked on large farms called plantations.

FAMOUS FIRSTS

- The first sawmill in America was built in Maine in 1623.
- America's first forest fire lookout station was set up near Greenville, on Squaw Mountain, in 1905.
- The first female American novelist, Sally Sayward Barrell (known as Madam Wood), was born in York, Maine.
- Maine was the first state to outlaw the sale of alcoholic beverages in 1851.
- Women in Maine were the first to vote. When women won the right to vote in 1920, Maine held its elections in September, before other states. This allowed women of Maine to use their right first.

By the 1800s, the issue of slavery was tearing apart the United States. Agriculture (farming) was the main way of life in the South, and Southerners depended on slaves to support their economy. In contrast, Northerners made a living not only by farming, but also by working in factories, where they were paid wages. They feared that if slavery were allowed throughout the country, Americans would lose jobs. As a result, many Northerners wanted to prevent the expansion of slavery. Antislavery feelings were strong in Maine, and efforts were made to abolish (put an end to) slavery.

Many African-Americans escaped from slavery by using the Underground Railroad. This was not a train, but a series of people and hideaways that helped slaves escape to the northern states and Canada, where they could be free. One hundred and two sites in 77 towns were located around Maine to help slaves make their way north.

THE CIVIL WAR

By the mid-1800s, tensions about slavery were about to boil over. North and South disagreed about whether new states admitted into the Union should be allowed to own slaves. Although the Missouri Compromise had addressed one crisis, the two sides would not be satisfied for long. To protect their rights, including the right to own slaves, Southerners banded together and seceded from, or left, the United States. They formed a new nation called the Confederate States of America.

In 1861, the Civil War broke out (1861–1865). Mill towns along the Kennebec and Androscoggin rivers boomed during the Civil War. Factories produced leather shoes, uniforms, and tents requested by the government to provide its army with necessities. Other Mainers served in the Union Army. About 73,000 Mainers fought for the North and thousands died. Maine contributed two great generals, Oliver Otis Howard and Joshua L. Chamberlain. In 1865 the Civil War ended and 8,000

Mainers had lost their lives. The North had won, and the slaves were freed.

THE TWENTIETH CENTURY

At the turn of the century, Maine faced severe competition in agriculture because of the rich soil and flat land in the west. Small farms began to decrease as farmers moved west and larger farms were created. Maine farmers adapted by turning to dairy, potatoes, and specialty crops such as apples and blueberries. When railroads started up in northern Maine in the late 1800s, Aroostook farmers gained easier access to other markets. The Aroostook Railroad was finished in 1894 and as a result, Aroostook County became one of the world's greatest potato-growing areas. The trains also helped Maine farmers to receive national recognition for their potato production.

Potato farming became big business in Maine during the late 1800s and early 1900s.

In 1929, crisis struck the nation. The Great Depression was a period of extremely low business activity that halted the entire country's economy. Many people lost money that they had invested in the stock market. People lost their jobs, banks closed, and farmers abandoned their farms. Many couldn't even afford to buy bare necessities such as bread. The Great Depression was very hard on Maine, as well as other states.

The start of World War II (1939–1945) helped to ease the Great Depression. Although the United States did not join the war until 1941, it provided goods and machinery to England, France, and other nations in the fight against Germany. Producing these necessities provided jobs and activity for workers across the United States. Maine factories made ships, and mills made shoes and uniforms for the soldiers. At Bath Iron Works in southern Maine, workers made 236 liberty ships during World War II. A liberty ship is a slow-moving cargo ship with the capacity to hold 11,000 tons.

After the war, tourism boomed. People from other states discovered that Maine's

A liberty ship, *Samuel Adams*, stands ready to be launched.

scenic coast was an ideal vacation spot. Hotels, resorts, and cottages began to spring up along the coast. The Maine Central Railroad opened a ticket office in New York. Advertisements persuaded people to visit Maine, and the economy began to flourish.

In the 1950s and 1960s, air force bases were built, electric companies came, and paper and food-packaging companies grew. Fish, french fries, and specialty crops such as blueberries and beans were packaged, frozen, and sold. The state's economy continued to improve as new service jobs were created at retail stores and restaurants. The population grew to 1,124,660, until a slow period of job activity called a recession hit Mainers. By 1993, more than 30,000 Mainers had lost their jobs.

In the 1960s, the Passamaquoddy Tribe and Penobscot Nation filed a lawsuit against the United States government. They claimed their land was taken from them illegally during the 1700s and 1800s, and they wanted the rights to some 12.5 million acres (5 million ha) of ancestral lands. The tribes rested their claims on law stating that the sale of Native American lands must first be approved by the United States Congress (the lawmaking body of the United States government). Since Congress hadn't approved it, the sale was invalid. In the 1980s, the government paid the Passamaquoddy and Penobscot tribes $81.5

WHAT'S IN A NAME?

The names of many places in Maine have interesting origins.

Name	Comes From or Means
Maine	Short for "mainland"; or named for a French province called Maine
Abenaki	Algonquian word for "people of the dawn" or "easterners"
Penobscot	Native American word meaning "place of rocks"
Katahdin	Maliseet word for "big mountain"
Allagash	Native American word for "bark-cabin lake"
Kennebec	Native American word for "long place of water"
Aroostook	Abenaki word for "beautiful river"

million for their land. Native Americans used the money to buy 300,000 acres (121,000 ha) of land, which they used to start a variety of businesses. Some of the land was turned into blueberry fields. Today, Native Americans are the second largest growers of blueberries in Maine.

MODERN TIMES

Many issues have arisen over the last thirty years in Maine. There is increasing concern about protecting the environment. Pollution has spilled from Maine's factories into the waters, killing many sea creatures. Environmentalists have helped to pass laws forcing paper companies and municipalities to improve the way in which they dispose of wastes. These laws have resulted in cleaner waterways in Maine.

Concerns about Maine's valuable forests being cut and damaged by insects raised numerous interests in the 1990s. Tree farms have been introduced to help protect the forests, but this issue still challenges the state. Other resources were also being depleted. In the mid to

This photo shows a blueberry field in Maine.

The massive lumber industry in Maine led to a need to protect Maine's natural resources.

late 1990s, a fishing boom led to overfishing, which resulted in smaller hauls.

Maine's Green Party has been fighting to protect fishing rights. Created in 1984, they are still hoping to restore the fish stocks as well as protect the economic and cultural industries of Maine's fishing and tourism sectors. The Green Party was the first official Green political organization in the United States. Their primary concern is protecting Maine's environment.

Maine's economy has always been tied to nature. The people of Maine are now working hard to find a way to preserve their environment. By preserving the environment, Mainers are managing the resources of their state and helping it to prosper. They are ensuring their future.

CHAPTER FOUR

GOVERNING MAINE

When Maine's constitution, or set of fundamental laws, was written in 1819, its creators weren't just thinking of the people living in the state at that time. They also thought about how the constitution would affect future Mainers. They must have done a good job—more than 180 years later, Maine still has the same constitution. In fact, Maine has one of the oldest constitutions of any state in the country. Of course, the constitution has been amended, or slightly changed, but it is still essentially the same.

The state government is organized in a way similar to that of the United States government. The constitution divides the government into three parts, or branches: the legislative branch, the executive branch, and the judicial branch. Each of these branches work together to help the state run smoothly.

The state government is centered around the capitol building in Augusta.

State representative Bernard McGowan stands in the newly renovated House chamber.

LEGISLATIVE BRANCH

The legislative branch creates laws, such as those to pay for schools and other public services, or to protect the environment. The legislature also approves the budget, a document produced by the governor to determine how the state's money will be spent. The people of Maine elect members of the legislative branch, called legislators, to serve for two-year terms.

The legislative branch consists of two parts, called houses: a 35-member senate and a 151-member house of representatives. Bills (proposed laws) may originate in either the senate or the house of representatives. If the house votes in favor of a bill, it is sent to the senate for approval and then to the governor to sign into law. If the governor does not approve a law, there must be a two-thirds majority in both houses in order to override (overturn) the governor's decision.

EXECUTIVE BRANCH

The executive branch is responsible for making sure that the laws in Maine are enforced and carried out. The governor is head of the executive branch. He or she is elected to a four-year term and may serve any number of terms, but not more than two consecutively (in a row). The governor has the power to call the senate and house of representatives into session, and to approve or reject bills.

Other officials in the executive branch include the secretary of state, the attorney general, and the state treasurer. The legislature elects each of these officials for a two-year term. The state auditor is also chosen by the legislature and serves a four-year term. The state auditor's duty is to study the state's financial records and report them to the legislature each year. Maine has no lieutenant governor.

JUDICIAL BRANCH

The judicial branch interprets, or explains, the laws and decides if someone has broken the law. The courts make up the judicial branch. Maine has three levels of courts: the supreme judicial court, superior court, and district and probate courts.

The supreme judicial court is the highest (most powerful) court in the state. It hears cases that are appealed from lower courts. An *appeal* is when a person asks for a higher court to review a decision made by a lower court. The supreme judicial court also oversees the conduct of lawyers and judges throughout the state. A chief justice (judge) and six

MAINE GOVERNORS

Name	Term	Name	Term
William King	1820–1821	Daniel F. Davis	1880–1881
William D. Williamson	1821	Harris M. Plaisted	1881–1883
Benjamin Ames	1821–1822	Frederick Robie	1883–1887
Daniel Rose	1822	Joseph R. Bodwell	1887
Albion K. Parris	1822–1827	Sabastian S. Marble	1887–1889
Enoch Lincoln	1827–1829	Edwin C. Burleigh	1889–1893
Nathan Cutler	1829–1830	Henry B. Cleaves	1893–1897
Joshua Hall	1830	Llewellyn Powers	1897–1901
Jonathan G. Hunton	1830–1831	John Fremont Hill	1901–1905
Samual E. Smith	1831–1834	William T. Cobb	1905–1909
Robert P. Dunlap	1834–1838	Bert M. Fernald	1909–1911
Edward Kent	1838–1839	Frederick W. Plaisted	1911–1913
John Fairfield	1839–1841	William T. Haines	1913–1915
Richard H. Vose	1841	Oakley C. Curtis	1915–1917
Edward Kent	1841–1842	Carl E. Milliken	1917–1921
John Fairfield	1842–1843	Frederic H. Parkhurst	1921
Edward Kavanaugh	1843–1844	Percival P. Baxter	1921–1925
David Dunn	1844	Ralph Owen Brewster	1925–1929
John W. Dana	1844	William Tudor Gardiner	1929–1933
Hugh J. Anderson	1844–1847	Louis J. Brann	1933–1937
John W. Dana	1847–1850	Lewis O. Barrows	1937–1941
John Hubbard	1850–1853	Sumner Sewall	1941–1945
William G. Crosby	1853–1855	Horace A. Hildreth	1945–1949
Anson P. Morrill	1855–1856	Frederick G. Payne	1949–1952
Samuel E. Wells	1856–1857	Burton M. Cross	1952–1953
Hannibal Hamlin	1857	Nathaniel M. Haskell	1953
Joseph H. Williams	1857–1858	Burton M. Cross	1953–1955
Lot M. Morrill	1858–1861	Edmund S. Muskie	1955–1959
Israel Washburn, Jr.	1861–1863	Robert N. Haskell	1959
Abner Coburn	1863–1864	Clinton A. Clauson	1959
Samuel Cony	1864–1867	John H. Reed	1959–1967
Joshua L. Chamberlain	1867–1871	Kenneth M. Curtis	1967–1975
Sidney Perham	1871–1874	James B. Longley	1975–1979
Nelson Dingley	1874–1876	Joseph E. Brennan	1979–1987
Seldon Connor	1876–1879	John R. McKernan, Jr.	1987–1995
Alonzo Garcelon	1879–1880	Angus S. King, Jr.	1995–

MAINE STATE GOVERNMENT

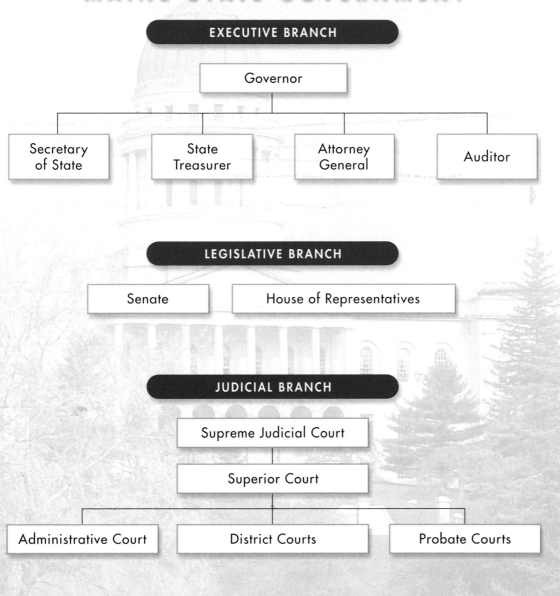

EXECUTIVE BRANCH

Governor

- Secretary of State
- State Treasurer
- Attorney General
- Auditor

LEGISLATIVE BRANCH

- Senate
- House of Representatives

JUDICIAL BRANCH

Supreme Judicial Court

Superior Court

- Administrative Court
- District Courts
- Probate Courts

associate justices serve on the supreme judicial court. The chief justice is head of the judicial branch. The governor appoints judges for a seven-year term.

The superior court is below the supreme judicial court. It handles all major cases using a jury, a group of people chosen to make a judgment based on the facts and evidence of a case. The chief justice of the supreme judicial court appoints all superior court judges. There is one judge per county, for a total of sixteen judges.

The district court handles divorce, juvenile offenders, and minor criminal and civil cases such as trespassing or traffic tickets. The governor appoints the 22 district court judges to a seven-year term. Probate courts handle wills, estates, and adoptions. One probate judge per county is elected by the people to serve for four years. Lastly, the administrative court in Portland serves the entire state. It hears cases involving the granting of various licenses by state agencies.

TAKE A TOUR OF AUGUSTA, THE STATE CAPITAL

Augusta is located in south central Maine, just one hour away from Maine's rocky coast and sandy beaches. Augusta replaced Portland as the capital in 1832 because it was more centrally located. Today, Augusta is the center of state government as well as the host of many business opportunities and services for central Maine. The 2000 census counted 18,560 people living in Augusta.

The first stop on our tour is the capitol building. Noted architect Charles Bulfinch designed it, and the first cornerstone was laid in 1829. The building was completed three years later. In 1911, most of the original structure was demolished and replaced with designs by G. Henri Desmond, who nearly doubled its size. Constructed of granite quarried from nearby Hallowell, the four-story white build-

Augusta is a scenic capital city along the Kennebec River.

ing features a graceful portico overlooking Capitol Park. With a 300-foot (91-m) front and two 75-foot (23-m) wings, the capitol exhibits a 185-foot (56-m) dome that rises above the city. Like a crown on the dome stands the magnificent statue of a woman called the Lady of Wisdom, holding a pine branch in her hand. The pine branch is a symbol of the Pine Tree State.

Inside the capitol, the governor meets with legislators and cabinet (staff) members. The most frequent visitors are students learning about Maine. Aside from seeing the governor's office, visitors can view historic portraits of former Maine governors, or take a stroll down the Hall of Flags. Bronze cases display the many captured battle flags collected during the Civil War. The display honors the military men and women who have served the state.

The Lady of Wisdom can be seen through a skylight in a tunnel connecting the State House to the state office building.

Not far from the capitol is Blaine House, former home of politician James G. Blaine. Blaine was a speaker of the United States House of Representatives in the mid-1800s. Since 1919, when his family donated the home to the state, the 28-room mansion has been the official home of Maine governors. Visitors can see early architecture designs from the 1800s or take a glimpse into where state leaders have lived.

The Maine State Museum contains exhibits devoted to Maine history, culture, and natural resources. You can learn about the history of Maine's lumbering and fishing industries. You'll also find out how early settlers removed ice from the rivers to sell, and how the state's earliest inhabitants lived. There are life-size mounts of many of Maine's animals in their natural settings, including the black bear and the bobcat. The museum also has a water-powered woodworking mill.

Next, visit the Children's Discovery Museum. The name of this museum says it all—it is a place to learn and discover while having fun. At the Children's Discovery Museum, you can pretend to work at a diner, a post office, or a grocery store. Visitors can also get involved in workshops and crafts.

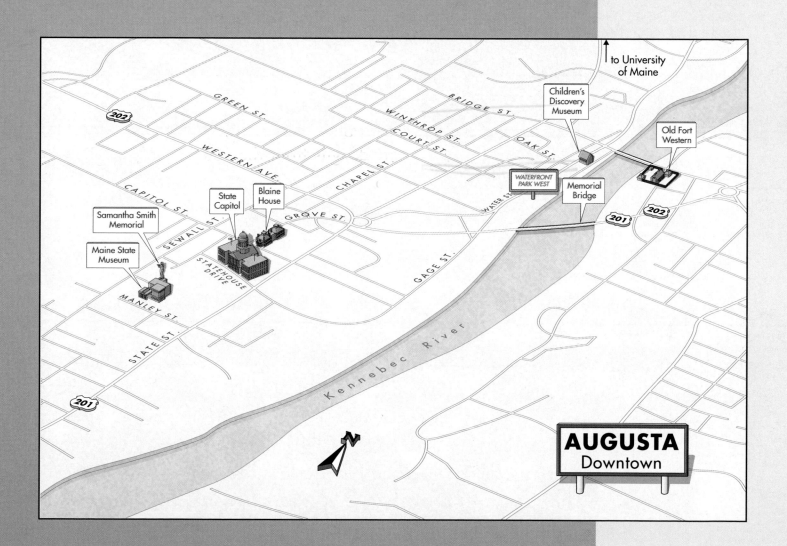

Then swing by the University of Maine's Augusta campus. Established in 1862, the University of Maine is the state's third largest university. It offers various programs to students across the state at seven locations, including the Augusta campus and the main campus in Orono. The University of Maine at Augusta is situated on 160 acres (65 ha) of woodlands. Students do not live at this campus, but they take classes there during the day and return home at night. The campus itself has an Architect and Performing Arts center, a bookstore, and a library, along with sports facilities such as soccer fields and basketball, tennis, and volleyball courts.

Our final stop is the Kennebec River, which divides the city in half. Located on the banks of the river is Old Fort Western. Built in 1754, it is America's oldest surviving wooden fort. Captain James Howard used this house as a command center, a store, and a family home from 1754 to 1767. For the next fifty years, the store served as a center of trade for settlers in Boston, New Foundland, and the West Indies. Today it is a national historic landmark. The staff re-create Old Fort Western by dressing in period costumes. Visitors can tour military, store, and house exhibits to get an idea of what life was like in Maine in the 1700s.

At Old Fort Western, guides and visitors dress in costume.

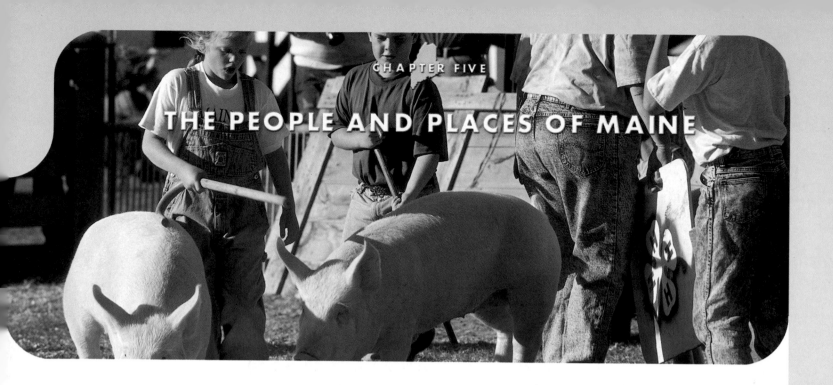

CHAPTER FIVE

THE PEOPLE AND PLACES OF MAINE

Two young children show off their pigs at the Fryeburg Fair.

According to the 2000 census, 1,274,923 people live in Maine. Maine is ranked 40th in population in the United States. About 97 in every 100 people in Maine are of European descent, including people from England, France, Canada, Ireland, and Italy. The rest are African-American, Asian, Hispanic, or Native American.

Although these minority groups are small, Maine is currently experiencing huge growth in racial diversity. Since 1990, its Asian and Hispanic populations have increased dramatically. The number of African-Americans is growing, as well. The Census Bureau predicts that this type of diversity will continue well into the future.

Acadians and French-Canadians make up a large part of the population. The Acadians were originally from a French colony in southeastern Canada. In 1763, the English drove the Acadians from Nova Scotia, Canada, and many of them settled in the St. John Valley (along the border of Maine). French-Canadians came from Quebec when Maine's lumber and textile industries increased after the Civil War. French is the primary language in most of the St. John Valley, and it is the second language in many of Maine's cities.

Native Americans were the first people on Maine's land. Today, 4,000 descendants of the Abenaki live on state reservations. The Penobscot live on Indian Island in the Penobscot River at Old Town, and the two Passamaquoddy reservations are in Washington County. The Micmac live in Aroostook County with headquarters in Presque Isle, and the Maliseet live near Houlton on an 800-acre (324-ha) tribal center.

Compared to most other states, the number of people who live in Maine is small. There are only 41 persons per square mile (16 per sq km) in crowded areas. This figure is known as the population density. (Compare that to New Jersey's population density of 80 people per square mile!) It also has one of the country's lowest crime rates, making it a very safe place to live.

A Maliseet Indian chief in traditional dress.

Almost half of Mainers live in cities or towns along the coast. Portland is the state's largest city, with 64,249 people. It is also the chief seaport and the closest United States port to Europe. Other large communities include Augusta, Bangor, and Lewiston. In the northern part of the state, you can get away from the busy cities and crowds; there's only about one person per square mile (one per sq km) in northern Maine.

Although Portland is the largest city in Maine, it still holds the charm of a small town.

WORKING IN MAINE

Maine has always relied on its natural resources, especially its 17 million acres of forests. Today, paper products bring in more money to Maine than any other product in the state. Newsprint, tissues, and paper towels are some of the paper products manufactured in Maine. Wood products are also important, including toothpicks, matches, and cardboard. Maine manufactures about 50 billion toothpicks per year. That's enough for every person on earth to have ten toothpicks each!

WHO'S WHO IN MAINE?

Leon Leonwood (L. L.) Bean (1873–1967) was an outdoorsman. He founded the nationally known L. L. Bean store, which sells outdoor gear and clothing. Bean was born in Greenwood.

At the paper mill, sheets of paper are covered with a coating and then dried.

Most people in Maine work in the service industry. These jobs include restaurant waiters, store clerks, teachers, doctors and nurses, and government employees. Together, service industries account for the largest amount of Maine's gross state product (the total value of all goods and services produced in the state in a year).

Only a small number of people farm in Maine because of the poor soil and short growing seasons. There are about 7,000 farms in the state, but most owners hold a second job to provide more income. Of the 1,270,000 acres (513,951 ha) classified as farmland, only three percent of the land is used to grow crops. In northwestern Maine, the soil is sandy but perfect for growing potatoes. Potatoes are the most valuable crop, and the state's output is ranked sixth in the nation. Other important farm products are milk and eggs. Maine also grows more blueberries than any other state. Apples and strawberries are other specialty crops (crops that are not available in every state, making them unique to Maine).

A young worker handpicks potatoes and sorts them into baskets and barrels.

Native Americans first harvested Maine blueberries. By the mid-1800s, berries were being canned and shipped to Union troops during the Civil War. Today, Maine is the largest producer of wild blueberries in the world. Wild blueberries are grown on more than 60,000 acres (24,281 ha) in Maine, and most are harvested and frozen. Try this simple and deliciously cold blueberry treat. Don't forget to ask an adult for help!

PATRIOTIC PIE

3-1/4 cups blueberry muffin mix
1/4 cup butter
4-1/2 cups vanilla ice cream
1 cup blueberries
1 cup strawberries, sliced

1. Preheat oven to 400° F. Grease 9-inch pie plate.
2. CRUST: Place muffin mix and butter in bowl. Mix well.
3. Spread evenly in ungreased 9-inch square baking pan. Do not press.
4. Bake at 400° F for 10 minutes. Stir. Set aside 1/2-cup crust mixture.
5. Press remaining crust mixture against bottom and sides of pie plate. Cool completely.
6. FILLING: Spread ice cream over crust. Sprinkle saved crust mixture on top.
7. Freeze until firm.
8. TOPPING: Place rinsed blueberries and strawberries on top of pie. Serve.

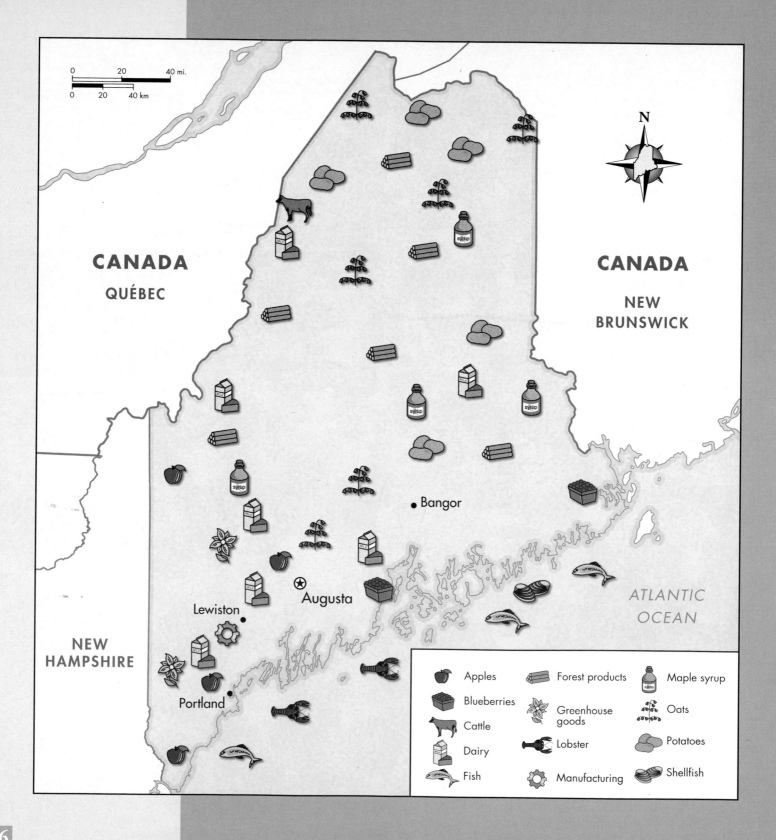

CANADA
QUÉBEC

CANADA
NEW BRUNSWICK

NEW HAMPSHIRE

• Bangor

⭐ Augusta

Lewiston •

Portland •

ATLANTIC OCEAN

🍎 Apples
🫐 Blueberries
🐄 Cattle
🥛 Dairy
🐟 Fish

🪵 Forest products
🌼 Greenhouse goods
🦞 Lobster
⚙ Manufacturing

🍁 Maple syrup
🌾 Oats
🥔 Potatoes
🦪 Shellfish

0   20   40 mi.
0   20   40 km

N

Fishing has been important since the colonial period. Maine is famous for its lobsters. Lobster boats and shacks are scattered along Maine's coast. Fishermen haul in approximately 57 million pounds of lobster each year, contributing $137 million to the state. Other catches include flounder, cod, clams, and shellfish. New techniques have enabled Maine to freeze its catches and transport them to other parts of the country. Maine's total fish catch per year averages more than $200 million.

Commercial lobstermen sort their harvest from Penobscot Bay.

Food processors are also important to Maine's economy. Vegetables, seafood, poultry, blueberries, and french fries are canned or frozen and sold elsewhere. These industrial areas are not grouped together centrally but are spread out among various counties. There are manufacturing or food processing plants in almost every county, including Kennebec, York, Androscoggin, and Cumberland.

Tourism also creates many jobs for Mainers. Visitors need accommodations, transportation, or information about Maine. Tourists spend money in hotels, restaurants, buses, museums, and attractions. More than 3 million people flock to Maine each year to view the scenic coastline, scattered islands, historic lighthouses, lakes, and mountains.

(TAKE A TOUR OF THE PINE TREE STATE)

Down East

Maine's beautiful northeastern coast stretches up to Lubec, the easternmost point of the United States. The first rays of sun hit Lubec each day before any other town in the country. Located on this easternmost point is one of Maine's 72 lighthouses. The 49-foot (15-m) red and white West Quoddy Head Lighthouse rises 83 feet (25 m) above water. It is the second most photographed lighthouse in the nation. (The nation's most photographed lighthouse is Heceta Head Lighthouse in Oregon.) The red and white stripes were painted to help ships see the light in winter. This 1858 lighthouse still works with a brightly shining beacon and loud foghorn. Visitors can look out from West Quoddy Head Lighthouse and see for miles.

(opposite)
West Quoddy Head Lighthouse is one of Maine's oldest lighthouses.

Down the coast in Machias, you will find the oldest building in eastern Maine, the Burnham Tavern. Built in 1770, this tavern served as a meeting place where plans were made for the first naval battle of the Revolutionary War. It displays artifacts and photographs that tell the story of how locals captured the British ship *Margaretta* on June 12, 1775.

Located on the rocky shore of Mount Desert Island is Acadia National Park. Much of the region's natural beauty is preserved in the park's 48,419 acres (19,603 ha). It is Maine's only national park, and the oldest park east of the Mississippi River. The mountains offer spectacu-

A hiker takes in the view from a hiking trail in Acadia National Park.

lar ocean views. Mount Cadillac is the highest at 1,200 feet (366 m). Activities include boating, biking, camping, rock climbing, horseback riding, hiking, or simply smelling the fresh salty air.

Another interesting place to visit on Mount Desert is the Oceanarium Lobster Hatchery in Bar Harbor. There you can see a different type of farming—lobster farming! Discover the fascinating life of a lobster and its environment. You can watch the daily routines of thousands of baby lobsters being hatched and raised for future release.

Mid Coast

Seaside resorts, fresh lobster, and charming fishing villages are all part of this region. If you happen to be in Rockland during August, you can enjoy the annual Maine Lobster Festival. Mainers celebrate the famed lobster with parades, live entertainment, boat rides, and great food. Lobster is cooked in the world's largest outside lobster pot or boiler. It is 24 feet (7.3 m) long and can steam 5,000 pounds (2,250 kg) of lobster every hour!

At Boothbay Harbor, visitors can enjoy a little bit of everything. Rent a coveside cottage, travel along village streets and peer into

Young Mainers participate in a lobster-eating contest at the Maine Lobster Festival.

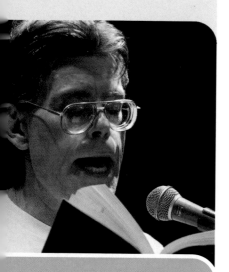

quaint shops, or watch lobster boats sailing out to sea. Boothbay Harbor is one of Maine's most refreshing areas.

Travel to Bath to visit what used to be Maine's largest private employer, Bath Iron Works. Bath Iron Works has been producing the finest steel ships since the 1800s, and at one time, it led the world in the production of wooden ships. Over the last century, battleships, frigates, and destroyers have been produced for the United States Navy at Bath. Visitors to the site can see the oldest surviving shipyard at the Marine Museum.

Maine's first state capital, Portland, is on the coast. It is also the largest seaport in the state. Boats travel in and out carrying fish, oil, and frozen foods. Located on the highest point in Portland is the 1807 Portland Observatory. A sea captain named Lemuel Moody built the tower in order to see ships coming in from a distance. Lemuel and his son, Enoch, used bright-colored flags to warn boats of approaching storms or signal to ships in distress.

The first public park in Portland was Lincoln Park. When the entire block burned down in the Great Fire of Portland in 1866, the city decided to turn it into a public park. They hoped that if there was another fire, the open space would prevent it from spreading. Today, you can enjoy a peaceful view there or get some exercise.

If you like baseball, stop by Hadlock Field, home of the Portland Sea Dogs. Join Slugger the Sea Dog, the team's official mascot, in cheering on the team. Off the field, Slugger can be found entertaining children at birthday parties, hospitals, and other places.

Also in Portland you can visit poet Henry Wadsworth Longfellow's home. He created his famous poems there. His is the oldest house on the Portland peninsula.

Southern Coast

Half of Maine's visitors come to the beautiful southern coast. Miles of white sandy beaches stretch along the coast. In Saco, children can learn about sea life at the Maine Aquarium. It exhibits live sharks, 250-pound (113-kg) seals, penguins, eels, and other marine creatures along with a 35-pound (16-kg) lobster! Learn about the creatures found among Maine's ponds, rivers, and salt marshes by checking out a duck pond or gazing into a 20,000-gallon (75,708-liter) fish tank.

Next, visit the villages of the Kennebunks: Kennebunk and Kennebunkport. These two charming towns are famous resort areas found side by side on the banks of Maine's southern coast. Former United States president George Bush spends his summers in Kennebunkport. The villages offer fine dining, golfing, cross-country skiing, and horseback riding.

A delicious site in Kennebunk is the Wedding Cake House, one of the most photographed homes in the nation. The pale yellow house is laced with gingerbread trim, carved spirals, and beautiful details that look like frosting on a cake. In the 1800s, shipbuilder George W. Bourne surprised his bride by decorating the house like a wedding cake. Now a private residence and bridal shop, this home is still a delight to see.

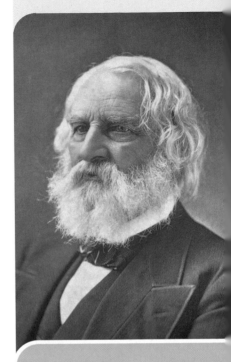

WHO'S WHO IN MAINE?

Henry Wadsworth Longfellow (1807–1882) was one of the most popular poets of his time. Educated at Maine's Bowdoin College, he later returned to the school as a teacher. After retiring in 1854, Longfellow devoted his time exclusively to writing. His works include *Evangeline*, *The Song of Hiawatha*, and *The Courtship of Miles Standish*. Longfellow was born in Portland.

The Wedding Cake House was originally built in 1826 by a shipbuilder. Years later he added lavish details for decoration.

Looming high on a hill in York is the Old Gaol. *Gaol* is an old English word for jail. The jail was built in 1719 to house debtors (people owing money), murderers, and thieves. To pass the time, criminals counted off the days by scratching numbers into the floor of their cell. These markings can still be viewed today. It would be hard to escape from the walls of the Old Gaol as they are 2 feet (.6 m) thick. The prison was converted into a museum in the 1900s and the cells, dungeon, and gaoler's quarters are still furnished as if it were 1790.

Our final destination in southern Maine includes shopping in Kittery. The Kittery Trading Post is found on the Maine-New Hampshire border. Purchased by Philip Adams in 1938 as a one-room trading post/gas station, he gained a reputation as an honest trader. He swapped furs for gas or beef for ammunition. Today, it is a 42,000-square-foot (3,902-sq-m) store where you'll find racks of clothes, canoes, and other outdoor items.

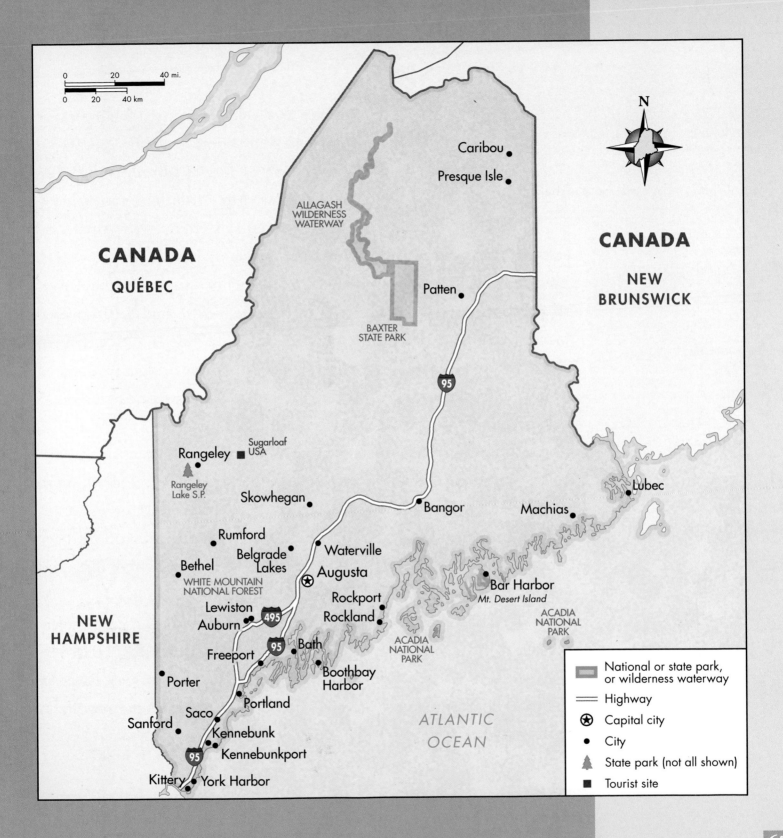

CANADA

QUÉBEC

CANADA

NEW BRUNSWICK

NEW HAMPSHIRE

ALLAGASH WILDERNESS WATERWAY

BAXTER STATE PARK

Caribou

Presque Isle

Patten

95

Rangeley

Sugarloaf USA

Rangeley Lake S.P.

Skowhegan

Bangor

Machias

Lubec

Rumford

Belgrade Lakes

Waterville

Bethel

WHITE MOUNTAIN NATIONAL FOREST

Augusta

Bar Harbor
Mt. Desert Island

ACADIA NATIONAL PARK

Rockport

Rockland

ACADIA NATIONAL PARK

Lewiston

Auburn

495

Porter

95

Bath

Boothbay Harbor

Freeport

Portland

Saco

Sanford

Kennebunk

95

Kennebunkport

Kittery

York Harbor

ATLANTIC OCEAN

N

0   20   40 mi.

0   20   40 km

National or state park, or wilderness waterway

Highway

Capital city

City

State park (not all shown)

Tourist site

Western Maine

For the nature lover, western Maine offers fewer cities and more country. Numerous lakes and dense forests surround this area. Head northwest to Porter to see an old covered bridge built in 1876. Early Americans started transporting goods across rivers by laying logs across the waters. To extend the length, they added trusses, arches, and eventually covers to prevent weather damage. At one time, Maine had 120 covered bridges; all but eight have been destroyed by fire, floods, or ice. One of the remaining bridges is the 152-foot (46-m) Porter Bridge. As a shared project, the bridge was constructed across the Ossipee River by residents of Porter and Parsonsfield.

Head north to the Rangeley Lakes, a popular vacation area, and discover 691 acres (280 ha) of accessible wilderness. There's something to do all year round in this region. Rangeley Lakes State Park offers camping or hiking among sparkling lakes surrounded by extraordinary mountains. Moose freely roam the area. In winter, snowmobiling and cross-country skiing on the trails is a favorite activity.

If you'd like to ski down the longest vertical drop in the East, Sugarloaf USA is the place to visit. It slopes vertically down for 2,028 feet (618 m) and offers 45 miles (73 km) of trails. The Sunday River in Bethel is another popular ski area, offering eight connected mountain peaks.

Central Maine

Many of Maine's major cities are in central Maine. Lewiston and Auburn, sometimes referred to as the Twin Cities, are located on opposite sides of the Androscoggin River. Lewiston is Maine's second largest city and is on the east bank. The city became known for its textiles and footwear. It is also home to Bates College, New England's first college to enroll both men and women. Auburn, on the west bank, has a population of 23,203.

Traveling to Waterville, there is very little evidence of human life before the 1600s. In 1802, eight hundred people officially formed the town of Waterville. In 2002, residents will celebrate the town bicentennial with parades, live performances, dancing, films, and music.

On Great Pond, visitors can enjoy an unusual activity—a ride on a pontoon boat with the letter carrier. Relax on a 30-foot (9-m) boat with a packed lunch and enjoy the natural beauty of Maine. The people who live in the area have their mail delivered to mailboxes placed on their docks.

Northern Maine

Bangor is Maine's third largest city and the gateway to the north woods. Just outside the city, families can stay at an 1840s farmhouse. Hamstead Farm offers a great opportunity for those who don't get the chance to spend time on a real farm. You can help feed the animals, hold a baby pig, or chase after a turkey.

Baxter State Park is 202,064 acres (81,772 ha) of wilderness land. A gift to Maine by former Governor Percival P. Baxter, he bought his first tract of land in 1930. A year later, Baxter gave the land to the state. Today it is a paradise for nature lovers, photographers, and mountain climbers. It includes 46 mountain peaks and ridges, miles of hiking trails, and 10 campgrounds.

The Patten Lumbermen's Museum is a good place to see one of the nation's best logging areas. Established in 1962, near the small town of Patten, the museum preserves the lumber industry as it evolved in northern Maine. Features include a working model of a sawmill, antique tractors, a blacksmith shop, and an 1820 logging camp. Thousands of artifacts from the logging industry allow visitors to get a feel for the history of this important Maine industry.

There's no better place to end a tour of Maine than at the Allagash Wilderness Waterway. This area of brooks, streams, and lakes is one of America's most beautiful and least-spoiled places. Paddle northward through the historic logging country, or race down crashing white

Canoeists take in the scenery on the Allagash River in northern Maine.

water to untamed areas of northern Maine. Continue if you dare around Attean Mountain to portage around Holeb Falls. To portage you must carry all your supplies on land—even your canoe! Stop and pick blueberries on lakeshores while you rest. If you're lucky you'll catch sight of a nesting bald eagle, a roaming moose, or a bear.

No matter where you are in Maine, you will never run out of things to do, places to go, or things to see. There is something for everyone in the Pine Tree State.

MAINE ALMANAC

Statehood date and number: March 15, 1820/23rd

State seal: A moose lying under a pine tree, with a farmer on one side and a sailor on the other. Adopted in 1820.

State flag: The Maine coat of arms on a blue background. Adopted in 1909.

Geographic center: Southern Piscataquis County, 18 miles (29 km) north of Dover-Foxcroft

Total area/rank: 33,741 square miles (87,389 sq km)/39th

Coastline: 613 square miles (1,588 sq km)

Borders: New Hampshire, Québec, New Brunswick, and the Atlantic Ocean

Latitude and longitude: Maine is located at approximately 45° N and 69° W

Highest/lowest elevation: Mount Katahdin, 5,367 feet (1,605 m)/Atlantic Ocean, sea level

Hottest/coldest temperature: 105° F (41° C) on July 10, 1911 at North Bridgton/–48° F (–44° C) on January 19, 1925 at Van Buren

Land area/rank: 30,865 square miles (49,654 sq km)/39th

Inland water area/rank: 2,263 square miles (5,861 sq km)/12th

Population (2000 census): 1,274,923/40th

Major cities (2000 census):

Portland: 64,249

Lewiston: 35,690

Bangor: 31,473

South Portland: 23,324

Auburn: 23,203

Origin of state name: Named to distinguish the mainland from offshore islands; also named after a province in France called Maine

State capital: Augusta

Counties: 16

State government: 35 senators, 151 representatives

Major rivers/lakes: Kennebec, Androscoggin, Penobscot, St. John, St. Croix, Piscataquis, Allagash, Machias, Aroostook/Moosehead, Sebago, Chesuncook, Chamberlain, Rangeley, Belgrade Lakes, and Grand Lakes

Farm products: Potatoes, blueberries, apples, milk, eggs, peas, apples, oats, maple syrup

Livestock: Beef cattle, poultry

Manufactured products: Paper, tissues, paper towels, cardboard, toothpicks, clothespins, lumber, furniture, shoes, boats, packaged foods, leather goods, electrical equipment, computers

Mining products: Sand and gravel, clay, garnets, limestone, peat, cement

Fishing products: Lobster, sardines, marine worms, shrimp, clams, flounder, cod

Animal: Moose

Berry: Wild blueberry

Bird: Chickadee

Cat: Maine coon cat

Fish: Landlocked salmon

Flower: White pine cone and tassel

Fossil: *Pertica quadrifaria*

Herb: Wintergreen (*Gaultheria procumbens*)

Insect: Honeybee

Mineral (Gemstone): Tourmaline

Motto: *Dirigo* (Latin for "I lead")

Nickname: The Pine Tree State or Down East

Song: "State of Maine Song," by Roger Vinton Snow

Tree: White pine tree

Wildlife: Bobcats, black bears, beavers, foxes, lynxes, marten, minks, racoons, puffins, white-tailed deer, bobcats, coyotes, foxes, skunks, minks, rabbits, squirrels, harbor seals, seagulls, eagles, owls, puffins, chickadees, ducks, loons

TIMELINE

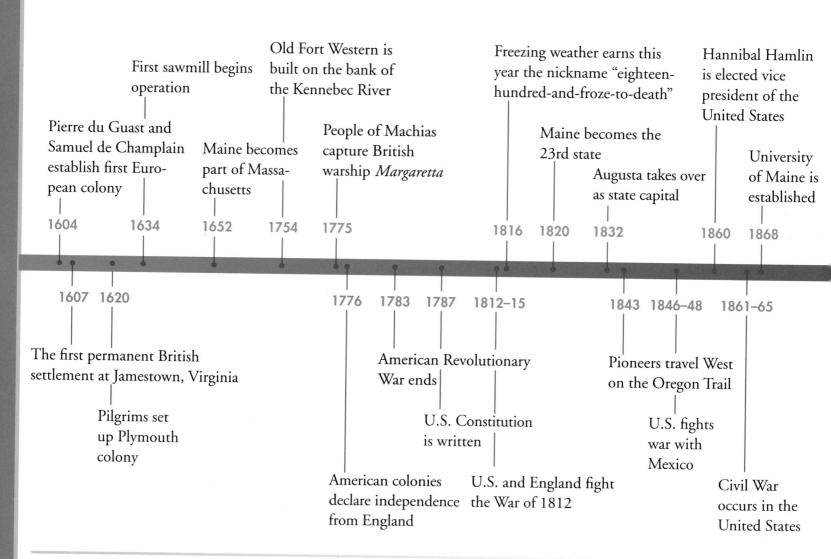

First sawmill begins operation

Old Fort Western is built on the bank of the Kennebec River

Freezing weather earns this year the nickname "eighteen-hundred-and-froze-to-death"

Hannibal Hamlin is elected vice president of the United States

Pierre du Guast and Samuel de Champlain establish first European colony

Maine becomes part of Massachusetts

People of Machias capture British warship *Margaretta*

Maine becomes the 23rd state

Augusta takes over as state capital

University of Maine is established

1604   1634   1652   1754   1775   1816   1820   1832   1860   1868

1607   1620   1776   1783   1787   1812–15   1843   1846–48   1861–65

The first permanent British settlement at Jamestown, Virginia

American Revolutionary War ends

Pioneers travel West on the Oregon Trail

Pilgrims set up Plymouth colony

U.S. Constitution is written

U.S. fights war with Mexico

American colonies declare independence from England

U.S. and England fight the War of 1812

Civil War occurs in the United States

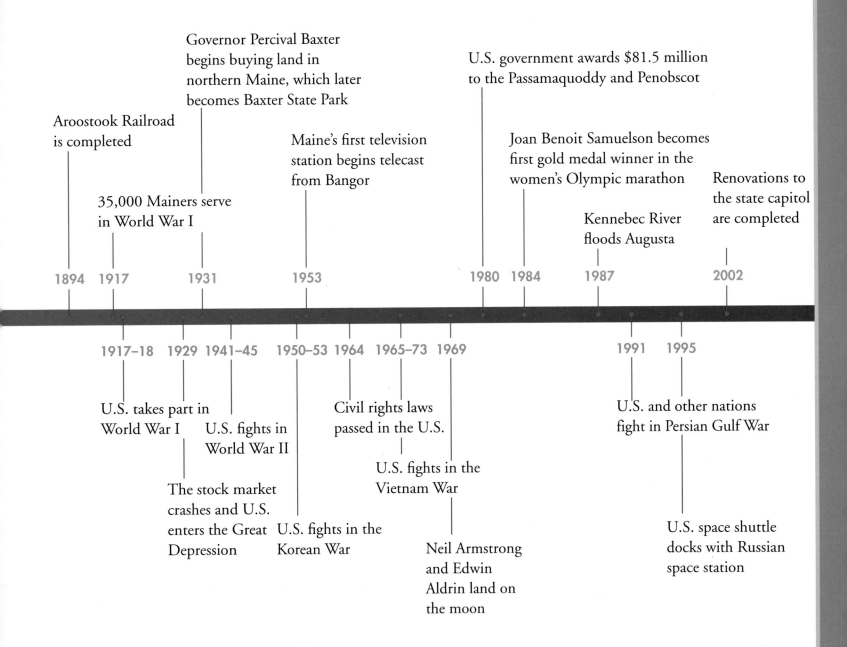

Governor Percival Baxter begins buying land in northern Maine, which later becomes Baxter State Park

U.S. government awards $81.5 million to the Passamaquoddy and Penobscot

Aroostook Railroad is completed

Maine's first television station begins telecast from Bangor

Joan Benoit Samuelson becomes first gold medal winner in the women's Olympic marathon

Renovations to the state capitol are completed

35,000 Mainers serve in World War I

Kennebec River floods Augusta

1894   1917   1931   1953   1980   1984   1987   2002

1917–18   1929   1941–45   1950–53   1964   1965–73   1969   1991   1995

U.S. takes part in World War I

Civil rights laws passed in the U.S.

U.S. and other nations fight in Persian Gulf War

U.S. fights in World War II

U.S. fights in the Vietnam War

The stock market crashes and U.S. enters the Great Depression

U.S. fights in the Korean War

Neil Armstrong and Edwin Aldrin land on the moon

U.S. space shuttle docks with Russian space station

GALLERY OF FAMOUS MAINERS

Milton Bradley
(1836–1911)
Developed games to encourage positive childhood development. His company, Milton Bradley, created popular games such as *Scrabble* and *Twister*. Born in Vienna.

Ricky Craven
(1966–)
Craven is a top competitor in NASCAR racing. Born in Newburgh.

Dorothea Dix
(1802–1887)
Taught in a Massachusetts school at age fourteen, and later helped to establish mental hospitals in several states. She worked as an advocate for the mentally ill and handicapped. Born in Hampden.

Hannibal Hamlin
(1809–1891)
First person from Maine to serve as vice president of the United States, under President Abraham Lincoln. Born in Paris Hill.

William King
(1768–1852)
Represented Maine in the General Court of Massachusetts and was a full supporter of Maine's separation. He later became the first governor of Maine when it entered the Union as the 23rd state. Born in Bath.

Edna St. Vincent Millay
(1892–1950)
One of the nation's most renowned twentieth-century poets. Works included *The Dream, The Wood Road,* and *The Poet and His Book*. Born in Rockland.

Joan Benoit Samuelson
(1957–)
Gold-medal winner in the inaugural women's marathon at the Summer Olympics in 1984. Born in Cape Elizabeth.

Liv Tyler
(1977–)
Actress whose films include *Armageddon* and *Stealing Beauty*. Born in Portland.

E. B. White
(1899–1985)
Award-winning children's book author. His books include *Stuart Little* and *Charlotte's Web*. Born in New York and lived in Allen Cove.

Andrew Wyeth
(1917–)
Modern artist whose work depicts everyday America, including entrancing images of Maine's landscapes and people. Spends summers in Cushing.

GLOSSARY

adapt: to adjust to something new

boycott: refusal to buy, sell, or trade with

charter: an official document or statement describing the rights and responsibilities of a city and its citizens

colonists: inhabitants of a colony

colony: settlement that is ruled by a distant country

conflict: a clashing of views or to struggle with

constitution: basic laws of a government

debt: something owed

dense: thick

economic: relating to production and use of goods and services

environmentalist: person who is concerned with protecting his or her surroundings

expedition: journey for the purpose of exploring

flourish: to thrive

hydroelectric: electricity produced by the motion of flowing water

manufacture: to produce or assemble

merchant: trader

pollute: contaminate

prehistoric: relating to a time known before history

preserve: protect

prominent: important

prosperous: to be successful

quarry: to dig from a quarry (place where stone is taken from earth)

recession: period in which there is slow business activity

reservation: public land set aside by government for use by Native Americans

resource: usable supply

tax: extra charges put on goods for the benefit of a state or country

textile: woven fabric

transport: to move goods by using ships, trains, boats, or cars

treaty: formal peace agreement between two or more groups

FOR MORE INFORMATION

Web sites

State of Maine

http://www.state.me.us
Official web site for the state of Maine.

Maine Secretary of State Kids' Page

http://www.state.me.us/sos/kids/homepage.htm
Useful information, games, and links for children about Maine.

Maine Office of Tourism

http://www.visitmaine.com
Information about Maine's regions, historic landmarks, and parks.

Maine History

http://resourcehelp.com/me_his.htm
Information and links about the history of Maine.

Books

Fazio, Wende. *Acadia National Park*. Danbury, CT: Children's Press, 1998.

Marsh, Carole. *Maine Timeline: A Chronology of Maine History, Mystery, Trivia, Legend, Lore and More*. Peachtree City, GA: Gallopade, 1994.

Marsh, Carole. *Maine Government for Kids*. Peachtree City, GA: Gallopade, 1999.

Woodson, Roger. *Family Adventure Guide: Maine*. Guilford, CT: Globe Pequot Press, 1997.

Addresses

Maine Publicity Bureau
97 Winthrop Street
Hallowell, ME 04347

Governor of Maine
Office of the Governor
#1 State House Station
Augusta, ME 04333–0001

INDEX

ABOUT THE AUTHOR

Christine Webster is an author of books for young readers. She has a special interest in United States and Canadian history. Her work for Children's Press includes titles in the series From Sea to Shining Sea and Cornerstones of Freedom, including *Pledge of Allegiance* and *Lewis and Clark*. She lives in Canada with her husband and three children.